John—The Gospel of Light and Life,
Revised and Expanded

(Adapted by permission from
The Light of Life Bible Correspondence Course
The Gospel of John)

*This is a self-study course
designed to help you discover
for yourself some important truths
from the gospel of John.*

how to study the lesson

1. Try to find a quiet spot free from distractions and noise.

2. Read each question carefully.

3. Look up the Scripture reference given after each question. Make sure you have found the correct Scripture passage. For example, sometimes you will find yourself looking up JOHN 1:1 instead of 1 JOHN 1:1.

4. Answer the question from the appropriate Bible passage. Write, in your own words, a phrase or sentence to answer the question. In questions that can be answered with a "yes" or "no" always give the reason for your answer... "Yes, because. . . ."

5. If possible, keep a dictionary handy in order to look up words you don't understand.

Copyright 1962, 1986 by THE MOODY BIBLE INSTITUTE OF CHICAGO
The author used the King James Version when preparing the questions for this manual

ISBN 0-8024-4375-3
7 Printing/EP/Year 91 90
Printed in the United States of America

6. Pray for God's help. You *need* God's help in order to understand what you study in the Bible. PSALM 119:18 would be an appropriate verse for you to take to God in prayer.

7. *Class teachers using this course for group study will find some helpful suggestions on page 63.*

how to take the self-check tests

Each lesson is concluded with a test designed to help you evaluate what you have learned.

1. Review the lesson carefully in the light of the self-check test questions.

2. If there are any questions in the self-check test you cannot answer, perhaps you have written into your lesson the wrong answer from your Bible. Go over your work carefully to make sure you have filled in the blanks correctly.

3. When you think you are ready to take the self-check test, do so without looking up the answers.

4. Check your answers to the self-check test carefully with the answer key given on page 64.

5. If you have any questions wrong, your answer key will tell you where to find the correct answers in your lesson. Go back and locate the right answers. Learn by your mistakes!

apply what you have learned to your own life

In this connection, read carefully JAMES 1:22-25. It is only as you apply your lessons to your own life that you will really grow in grace and increase in the knowledge of God.

The Deity of Jesus Christ

JOHN, chapter 1

God's Revelation: "The Word Was God" (1:1-18)

John describes Jesus Christ as the Light of Life. "In him was life; and the life was the light of men." 1:4

The "Word" of verse 1 is the eternal Son of God, Who took upon Himself flesh and blood (1:14) in order to reveal to us the true character of God (1:18) and in order to give light to all men (1:4).

1. How many times do the following words appear in John 1:1-18?

Believe _____   Light _____

Life _____   Word _____

2. What did "the Word" of verse 1 become?

1:14 _____

3. Whom did Jesus reveal?

1:18 _____

4. Who was the light of men?

1:4 _____

5. What must one do in order to become a son of God?

1:12 _____

Would you like to see the glory, the righteousness, the wisdom and the grace of God? You will see all of this and more if you will give yourself wholeheartedly to the study of the life of Christ in these lessons. God, who revealed portions of His truth in many ways to men by the prophets, has in these last days spoken to us by His Son, Jesus Christ.

6. By whom did God's law come into the world?

1:17 _____

By whom did grace and truth come?

1:17 _____

7. The new birth is distinct from natural birth. It is not the result of any human achievement. What, then, is its source?

1:13 _____

8. Through whom has the invisible God revealed Himself?

1:18 _____

John's Witness: "Behold the Lamb" (1:19-51)

We see here the testimony of John the Baptist concerning the Lord Jesus, and also the attraction of certain disciples to Christ.

9. When John said concerning himself, "I am the voice of one crying in the wilderness," from what Old Testament prophet was he quoting?

1:23 _____

10. What was John's testimony concerning Jesus?

1:29 _____

11. In what form did John see the Spirit descend on Jesus?

1:32 _____

4

12. John referred to Jesus as the Lamb of God (1:29). What additional title did he give to Him?

1:34 _____

13. What testimony did Andrew give concerning Jesus?

1:41 _____

14. What Old Testament writers spoke of Jesus of Nazareth?

1:45 _____

15. With what words did Jesus describe Nathaniel's character?

1:47 _____

16. Nathanael, in turn, gave three titles to Jesus. What were they?

1:49 a. _____ b. _____ c. _____

Ancient Jewish prophets foretold that a messenger would arrive before Christ, the world-Redeemer, to prepare the way for Him. John the Baptist was that promised messenger. To prepare men's hearts for Christ, John commanded them to repent of their sins. Those who repented he baptized in the Jordan River.

NOTE:

The Levites were members of the tribe of Levi who assisted the priests. 1:19

Elias (Elijah) was an Old Testament prophet whom the Jews expected would return. 1:21

Esaias (Isaiah) was a Jewish prophet. 1:23

Pharisees were members of a strictly orthodox religious party of the Jews. 1:24

Son of man was a term Jesus applied to Himself because, though truly God, He assumed human likeness to accomplish our salvation. 1:51

Prayer: O God, through this study bring light into my life. Help me to know, to love, and to serve Thee. Amen.

check-up time No. 1

You have just studied some important truths about John 1. Review your study by rereading the questions and your written answers. If you wish, you may use the self-check test as an aid in reviewing your lesson. If you aren't sure of an answer, reread the Scripture portion given to see if you can find the answer. Then take this test to see how well you understand important truths you have studied.

In the right-hand margin write "True" or "False" after each of the following statements.

1. John said, "Behold the Son of God which taketh away the sin of the world." _____

2. John said, "I saw, and bare record that this is the Son of God." _____

3. John baptized with the Holy Spirit. _____

4. The Pharisees asked John why he was baptizing. _____

5. John admitted that he was Elias. _____

6. John saw the Spirit descending like a dove. _____

7. Andrew brought his brother Philip to Jesus. _____

8. Moses and the prophets wrote about Jesus of Nazareth. _____

9. Nathanael said to Christ, "Thou art the Son of God." _____

10. Jesus said to Nathanael, "I saw thee under the fig tree." _____

Turn to page 64 and check your answers.

Signs and Salvation

JOHN, chapters 2 and 3

The Sign: "A New Wine" (2:1-25)

The disciples were attracted to the Light, the Lord Jesus Christ, by the testimony of John the Baptist. They brought others to Him by their own testimony. Some men were attracted to the Light by the "signs" that Jesus did.

The miracle at the wedding in Cana was the first of Jesus' miracles or "signs," and showed His divine power. The apostle John tells us that the signs that he recorded were included in his gospel for a definite purpose. (John 20:30-31)

1. Who were called to the wedding at Cana?

2:2 _____

2. What did Jesus' mother say to the servants at the wedding?

2:23 _____

3. How did this miracle of turning water into wine affect the disciples?

2:11 _____

Some time after this miracle Jesus went to Jerusalem, where He cleansed the Temple. That involved Him in a discussion with the Jews in which He revealed an important truth about His body.

4. Into what were the people turning God's Temple?

2:16 _____

5. What startling claim did Jesus make for Himself?

2:19 _____

6. What did He mean by such a claim?

2:21 _____

7. What had to take place before the disciples understood this remark?

2:22 _____

8. What happened to many who saw Jesus' miracles?

2:23 _____

9. Why did Jesus refuse to commit Himself unto men?

2:24 _____

The Salvation: "A New Birth" (3:1-36)

In John's Gospel we will see Christ denouncing religious hypocrites who have no sincere desire for truth. We will see Him showing infinite and loving patience with sincere inquirers, or even "honest doubters." In chapter 3 we have one of the most famous of Christ's discourses with an individual in his conversation with Nicodemus.

10. What was the religious rank of Nicodemus?

3:1 _____

11. What dogmatic statement did Jesus make to this religious leader?

3:3 _____

12. Nicodemus did not understand the new birth. With what words did he admit that?

3:9 _____

13. What Old Testament illustration did Jesus use to suggest His coming crucifixion?

3:14 _____

14. What well-known words explain the gospel?

3:16 _____

15. Why did God send His Son into the world?

3:17 _____

16. What is God's basis for condemnation?

3:18 _____

Nicodemus was a highly placed religious leader who recognized that the ministry of Jesus Christ was approved of God. He was attracted to Jesus by His miracles. The Lord Jesus swept aside that half-hearted belief and told Nicodemus that nothing less than a new start would do. That new start is expressed in the words "Ye must be born again."

17. Why do men love darkness rather than light?

3:19 _____

18. According to John the Baptist, from where does true authority come?

3:27 _____

19. With what words did John express his relationship to Jesus?

3:30 _____

20. How many things has the Father given to the Son?

3:35 _____

21. "He that believeth on the Son hath

_____ 3:36a

22. "He that believeth not the Son

_____ 3:36b

You will note that *believe, light,* and *life* are important words in this chapter. How many times does the word *believe* (include *believed* and *believeth*) occur? _____

check-up time No. 2

You have just studied some important truths about John 2 and 3. Review your study by rereading the questions and your written answers. If you aren't sure of an answer, reread the Scripture portion given to see if you can find the answer. Then take this test to see how well you understand the important truths you have studied.

In the right-hand margin write "True" or "False" after each of the following statements.

1. Jesus was invited to a marriage feast in Jerusalem. _____

2. Turning the water into wine was the first miracle recorded by John. _____

3. Jesus went to Jerusalem for the Feast of Tabernacles. _____

4. Peter poured out the changers' money and overthrew the tables. _____

5. Many believed in His name when they saw the miracles. _____

6. Nicodemus was a Pharisee. _____

7. Jesus said that unless you belong to a church you cannot see the Kingdom of Heaven. _____

8. Moses lifted up a golden serpent in the wilderness. _____

9. John was still baptizing at this time. _____

10. John admitted he was not the Christ. _____

Turn to page 64 and check your answers.

Water and Witness

JOHN, chapters 4 and 5

The Living Water: "Everlasting Life" (4:1-54)

The teaching of Jesus concerning women would entitle Him to rank with the great teachers of the world. When Jesus shared His deepest teaching with women, He was breaking with the customs of His day.

1. What phrase in 4:6 suggests the humanity of Jesus?

4:6 _____

2. Because the Jews had no dealings with the Samaritans, it was an act of humility for Jesus to ask the Samaritan woman for what?

4:7 _____

3. In return Jesus offered what to her?

4:10 _____

4. How would you evaluate the morals of this woman?

4:18 _____

5. How did she try to change the subject when faced with her sin?

4:20 _____

Notice that the Lord Jesus made the woman face the fact that she was a sinner. Confession of sin and true repentance are the first step toward a right relationship with God. The living water cannot flow until sin is taken out of the way.

The Samaritans were descendents of Jews and foreigners who inter-married. 4:9

Mt. Gerizim is the place at which Samaritans worshipped. 4:20 "Sal-vation is of the Jews" means that the Bible and Christ came through the Jews. 4:22

6. The Samaritan woman's first expression of faith in the person of Christ was expressed in what words?

4:19 _____

7. In what words did Jesus tell her that how we worship God is more important than where we worship Him?

4:24 _____

8. She finally expressed her faith in Christ to her own people. That expression was in the form of a question. What was it?

4:29 _____

Verse 24 of this chapter is very important. *Memorize* the verse.

9. For what two reasons did many of the Samaritans in Sychar believe on Jesus?

4:39 _____

4:41 _____

10. Jesus told His disciples that His "meat" was to do what?

4:34 _____

The second miracle that John records is the healing of the nobleman's son. The nobleman "believed the words that Jesus spoke unto him." Faith is vital for those who want to receive a blessing from Jesus.

11. What request did the nobleman (ruler) make of Jesus?

4:47 _____

13

12. What was Jesus' response?

4:50 _____

13. What were the results of the nobleman's obedience?

4:51 _____

4:53 _____

A Living Witness: "A Work and a Word" (chapter 5)

The third miracle was the healing of the man ill for thirty-eight years. The critics of Jesus persecuted Him for healing on the Sabbath day. The Sabbath was one day in seven set aside for rest and worship. The Jews rose in opposition when Jesus told the man to pick up his bed and walk.

14. What question did Jesus ask the impotent man?

5:8 _____

15. What command did He give him?

5:8 _____

16. On what day did this miracle take place?

5:9 _____

17. What warning did Jesus give this man after he was healed?

5:14 _____

Jesus defended Himself by saying that the work of God continues on the Sabbath. That angered the Jews still more because they recognized that Jesus was claiming to be equal with God.

18. For what two reasons did the Jews attempt to kill Jesus?

5:18 a. _____

   b. _____

19. How did Christ explain the way of salvation?

5:24 _____

Jesus met the charge of blasphemy with a statement regarding His relationship to God the Father (5:19-23). He then claimed to be Mediator, One who stands between God and men (5:24-29). The co-equality of God the Father and God the Son is such that, "He who does not honour the Son does not honour the Father who sent Him."

21. To whom has the Father committed all judgment?

5:22 _____

22. What persons or things bear witness that the Father has sent Him?

a. 5:33 _____

b. 5:36 _____

c. 5:37 _____

d. 5:39 _____

23. If the Jews had believed Moses, whom else would they have believed?

5:46 _____

check-up time No. 3

You have just studied some important truths about John 4 and 5. Review your study by rereading the questions and your written answers. If you aren't sure of an answer, reread the Scripture portion given to see if you can find the answer. Then take the following test to see how well you understand the important truths you have studied.

In the right-hand margin write "True" or "False" after each of the following statements.

1. Jesus met the Shunammite woman at the well. _____

2. Jesus said that He would give her "living water." _____

3. Those who worship God must worship in silence and in church. _____

4. Many of the Samaritans believed on Jesus. _____

5. Jesus healed the nobleman's son without going to his house. _____

6. The impotent man wanted to be healed in the pool of Salome. _____

7. Jesus found the healed man in the Temple later that day. _____

8. God has committed all judgment unto the Son. _____

9. There was no greater witness to Christ than that of John the Baptist. _____

10. The Scriptures did not testify to Christ. _____

Turn to page 64 and check your answers.

Manna and Mystery

JOHN, chapters 6 and 7

Manna: "Bread of Life" (chapter 6)

A great multitude followed Jesus when they saw that He healed the sick. On a mountainside Jesus performed another miracle. He fed a great crowd of more than 5,000 people with five loaves and two fishes. The people wanted to make Jesus king.

1. How many times do the following words occur in chapter 6?

a. Believe (includes *believed*) _____

b. Life _____

2. Why did Jesus ask Philip, "Whence shall we buy bread, that these may eat?"

6:6 _____

3. How much food remained after Jesus fed the multitude?

6:13 _____

4. In the lives of some this miracle produced a positive result. What was it?

6:14 _____

5. What words of assurance and comfort did Jesus give to His disciples during a stormy night on the sea?

6:20 _____

The next day the multitude followed Jesus again because they ate the loaves and were filled. Jesus wanted them to be concerned about food for their souls. He said, "I am the bread sent down from heaven. Feed upon me and you will have eternal life."

6. There are more reasons than one for following Jesus. Name one.

6:26 _____

7. What answer did Jesus give to the question, "What shall we do that we might work the works of God?"

6:29 _____

8. Of whom was Jesus speaking when He said, "The bread of God is He which cometh down from heaven"?

6:35 _____

9. Name one vital reason for which Jesus came down from heaven.

6:38 _____

10. What is the "Father's will," as suggested in verses 39 and 40?

6:39 _____

6:40 _____

11. How many of those who come to Christ will be cast out?

6:37 _____

12. What does Jesus make for Himself in 6:48?

6:48 _____

The people had never heard anyone talk like that before. Some said, "This is a hard saying." And "from that time many of his disciples went back, and walked no more with Him." (6:66)

Prayer: Lord, teach me to spend my effort on things that will endure unto everlasting life, rather than being concerned for things that will perish with this life. Amen.

13. How long had Jesus known who would really believe in Him?

6:64 _____

14. Of whom did Jesus say, "One of you is a devil?"

6:70 _____

Mystery: *"Who Is This man?"* (chapter 7)

The Jews believed that when the promised Messiah came He would become their king. When they saw Jesus feed the multitude, they thought, *This is the kind of king we want.*

As more and more of the common people became convinced that Jesus was the Christ, the Messiah, the Jewish leaders became more and more alarmed. They did not want a new king. The priests and Pharisees were jealous about their authority and positions of power, and they were afraid they might lose those if they had a new ruler. Jesus wanted to bring men and women into the Kingdom of God. He did not want to be an earthly King.

15. Why does the world hate Christ?

7:7 _____

16. What promise does Christ give to those who will do His will?

7:17 _____

17. What claim did Jesus make concerning His relationship with the Father?

7:33 _____

18. What did Christ promise to those who believed in Him?

7:38-39 _____

19. Many people were led to believe that Jesus was a

_____. 7:40

Others said He was the _____. 7:41

20. What did the officers who were sent to take Jesus captive say of Him?

7:46 _____

In this chapter we have found Jesus again in Jerusalem at the Feast of Tabernacles. The city was thronged with people who had come from all over Palestine for the religious holiday. There was much controversy over the Lord Jesus. Some said that He was the Christ and others that He was a deceiver. In this chapter we see the enmity of the religious leaders to Jesus. That enmity would grow until they finally succeeded in having Him crucified.

Prayer: O God, give me courage to be fair in my judgments, and give me wisdom to judge aright. Amen.

check-up time No. 4

You have just studied some important truths about John 6 and 7. Review your study by rereading the questions and your written answers. If you aren't sure of an answer, reread the Scripture portion given to see if you can find the answer. Then take the following test to see how well you understand important truths you have studied.

In the right-hand margin write "True" or "False" after each of the following statements.

1. The lad had enough food to feed 5,000 people. _____

2. The disciples entered into a ship and headed for Capernaum. _____

3. Jesus walked on the sea to the disciples' ship. _____

4. Jesus said that when the Holy Spirit came He would give them the bread of life. _____

5. After the Lord's parable about the bread many more followed Him. _____

6. Jesus chose eleven disciples. _____

7. Jesus went up to the Feast of the Tabernacles alone. _____

8. Most of the people were willing to give a testimony for Jesus. _____

9. The living water is the Holy Spirit within a believer. _____

10. None of the people ever considered Jesus to be a prophet. _____

Turn to page 64 and check your answers.

Light and Sight

JOHN, chapters 8 and 9

The Light: "I Am the Light of the World."
(chapter 8)

Chapter 8 opens with the story of the woman taken in adultery. The religious leaders brought her case to Jesus in order to trap Him. The woman's act was sinful, but Christ would not allow men who were themselves sinful to point out the woman's guilt while covering their own.

1. According to Mosaic law, what judgment was to be brought on a woman taken in adultery?

8:5 _____

2. Why did the scribes and Pharisees bring the woman to Christ?

8:6 _____

3. What did Jesus say to those who wanted her stoned?

8:7 _____

4. How many were apparently convicted of personal sin by Christ's censor?

8:9 _____

5. What does Christ say to those who are willing to turn from their sin?

8:11 _____

To the woman He said, "Go and sin no more." To all who come to Him He says the same. He is the Light of the world, come to dispel the darkness of sin. Light reveals dirt and uncleanness. It also cleanses. The holiness of Christ is a rebuke to man's sin; His power cleanses from sin. Jesus, the Light of the world, can lighten even the darkness of death.

6. What astounding claim did Jesus make

For Himself? _____ 8:12

For those who follow Him? _____ 8:12

7. If the Jews had known who Jesus was, whom else would they have known?

8:19 _____

8. What did Christ say about those who commit sin?

8:34 _____

9. How free from sin does Christ set those who accept Him as their personal Savior?

8:36 _____

10. Jesus described the devil as being what?

8:44 a. _____ b. _____

11. How did Jesus compare Himself to Abraham?

8:58 _____

The Sight: "Now I see" (chapter 9)

In chapter 8 Jesus claims to be the Light of the world. In chapter 9 He repeats the claim, and then proves it by giving sight to a man born blind. Jesus has power to give both physical sight and spiritual sight.

12. Why had this man been born blind?

9:3 _____

13. Jesus told the blind man to go to the pool and wash. What happened when he obeyed?

9:7 _____

14. On what day of the week did Christ heal this man?

9:14 _____

15. Why did some of the Pharisees believe that Jesus was not of God?

9:16 _____

16. What was the blind man's testimony concerning all of this?

9:25 _____

17. What pointed question did the healed man put to Christ's critics?

9:27 _____

The price of accepting Christ is sometimes high. The man who accepted Jesus' gift was cast out of the Temple. After reading this chapter, decide whether you think he believed the price was worth paying.

18. What was his attitude toward Christ when he discovered His true identity?

9:38 _____

19. What did Christ say about the sin of the religious Pharisees?

9:41 _____

Fill in the missing words:

20. Then spake Jesus again unto them, saying, _____

_____: he that followeth me shall not walk in darkness,

but shall have the _____ 8:12

21. Then said Jesus to those Jews which believed on Him,

If ye _____, then are ye _____

_____ 8:31

22. As long as I am in the world, I am _____

_____ 9:5

23. Some said, _____: others said _____:

but he said, _____ 9:9

24. He answered and said, "Whether he be a sinner or no, I know

not: _____

_____, that, whereas I was blind, _____ 9:25

The attitude of the Pharisees should teach us to be very careful to be loyal to the truth. Their religiousness was mere outward show. They had already decided that they did not want Christ.

They did not recognize Him as the Son of God, because if they did so they would logically have to serve and honor Him. They shut their eyes to the truth, so they really were the ones who were blind.

Are your eyes open? Are you eagerly looking for the truth of God?

Prayer: Create in me a clean heart, O God, and renew a right spirit within me. O God, give me wisdom to decide and courage to make a decision. Amen.

check-up time No. 5

You have just studied some important truths about John 8 and 9. Review your study by rereading the questions and your written answers. If you aren't sure of an answer, reread the Scripture portion given to see if you can find the answer. Then take the following test to see how well you understand important truths you have studied.

In the right-hand margin write "True" or "False" after each of the following statements.

1. Jesus condemned the woman who was taken in adultery.   _____

2. Jesus said, "If ye had known me ye should have known my Father also."   _____

3. A person can be a true disciple of Christ and at the same time ignore the Word of God.   _____

4. Christ said that the law of Moses could set men free from sin.   _____

5. Abraham rejoiced to see the day of the Messiah, Jesus Christ.   _____

6. Jesus commanded the blind man to wash in the pool of Bethesda.   _____

7. The young man was born blind.   _____

8. The Pharisees appreciated the testimony of the young man.   _____

9. The Pharisees cast the young man out of the Temple.   _____

10. Jesus made Himself known to the young man.   _____

Turn to page 64 and check your answers.

Shepherd and Savior

JOHN, chapters 10 and 11

The Shepherd: "The Good Shepherd" (chapter 10)

In the Bible, God's care for His people is very often likened to the care of a shepherd for his sheep. Jesus speaks of Himself as the Door of the sheepfold. "I am the Door: by me if any man enter in, he shall be saved, and shall go in and out, and find pasture." This is the third "I AM."

1. What claim did Jesus make for Himself?

10:7 _____

2. What happens to the person who enters the sheepfold by the Door (Jesus)?

10:9 _____

3. What kind of life does the Good Shepherd give His sheep?

10:10 _____

4. What did He have to do before He could give us that life?

10:11 _____

5. Who are the "other sheep" referred to in 10:16?

_____

6. Was Christ's death an accident?

10:17-18 _____

27

He is not only the Door of the sheepfold but is also the Good Shepherd who cares for the sheep. This is the fourth "I AM." The Good Shepherd gives His life for the sheep.

7. What claims did Jesus make about His sheep?

10:27 _____

8. What kind of life did He claim to give to them?

10:28 _____

9. With what words did Jesus claim deity?

10:30 _____

Jesus was walking in a porch of the Temple when He made that statement, and it so angered the Jews that they wanted to kill Him. Several times before, the Jews had wanted to kill Jesus and always for the same reason—He made Himself equal with God. In their minds there was no doubt about who He claimed to be.

10. While some persecuted and reviled Jesus, others did what?

10:42 _____

The Savior: "I Am the Resurrection and the Life" (chapter 11)

"The wages of sin is death." Because all have sinned, all must be prepared to die. Death holds no real fear for the man or woman who knows Jesus Christ as Savior and Lord. Jesus has tasted death for every man and has removed its sting by Himself conquering death. And to the believer He says, "Because I live, ye shall live also."

11. What did the Lord say of the sickness of His friend Lazarus?

11:4 _____

12. Why did Jesus not go and restore Lazarus before he died?

11:15 _____

13. How many days had Lazarus been dead when Jesus arrived in Bethany?

11:17 _____

14. With what words did Martha express her faith?

11:22 _____

15. Jesus makes an amazing claim in this chapter. What is it?

11:25 _____

In chapter 11 we see Jesus' power over death in the calling back to life of Lazarus, who had been dead four days. This is the seventh sign that John records, and it is in some ways the greatest of miracles. In the raising of Lazarus, Jesus showed that He is the giver of life.

16. Mary went out to meet Jesus. What did she do when she saw Him?

11:32 _____

17. What did Jesus say to Martha when she hesitated to obey His order to remove the stone?

11:40 _____

18. How did Jesus prove His claim to be the resurrection and the life?

11:43-44 _____

19. What were the two reactions to Lazarus's returning to life?

11:48 _____

Complete the following sentences:

20. And when he putteth forth his own sheep _____,

and the sheep follow him: _____ 10:4

21. I am the _____, and know my sheep,

and am _____ 10:14

22. And other sheep I have which are not _____.

them also I must _____, and they shall hear my voice;

and there shall be _____ fold, and _____ shepherd. 10:16

23. But ye believe not, because ye _____, as
I said unto you. 10:26

24. She saith unto him, "Yea, Lord: I believe that _____

_____ which should come into the world. 11:27

25. Then many of the Jews which came to Mary, and had seen

the things which Jesus did, _____ 11:45

To Martha, Jesus said: "I am the resurrection and the life; he that
believeth in me, though he were dead, yet shall he live: And whosoever liveth and believeth in me shall never die." This is the fifth
great "I AM." These are words that mankind, with a fear of the
grave, longs to hear. How faith rejoices that the Lord Jesus proved
His tremendous claim by raising the dead.

Prayer: Dear Lord, help me to believe Thy promise that those
who believe in Thee, though they may die, yet shall live. Amen.

check-up time No. 6

You have just studied some important truths about John 10 and 11. Review your study by rereading the questions and your written answers. If you aren't sure of an answer, reread the Scripture portion given to see if you can find the answer. Then take the following test to see how well you understand important truths you have studied.

In the right-hand margin write "True" or "False" after each of the following statements.

1. Jesus said that His sheep will hear His voice. _____

2. Jesus as the Good Shepherd laid down His life for the sheep. _____

3. Jesus predicted that the mobs in Jerusalem would take His life from Him. _____

4. The Jews believed what Jesus told them about the Good Shepherd. _____

5. The Jews had spears in their hands to kill Jesus. _____

6. Jesus went to Bethany immediately when He heard of the sickness of Lazarus. _____

7. The disciples hesitated about going back to Judaea. _____

8. Mary was the first one to go and meet Jesus. _____

9. Martha confessed that Jesus was the Christ, the Son of God. _____

10. The high priest prophesied that Jesus should die for the nation. _____

Turn to page 64 and check your answers.

Welcome and Washing

JOHN, chapters 12 and 13

The Welcome: "Hosanna: Blessed Is the King" (chapter 12)

Six days before the Passover, Jesus once more visited Bethany where Lazarus lived with his two sisters. The gratitude of the sisters who had received their brother back from the dead could not be measured. Mary tried to express her gratitude by anointing Jesus' feet with costly oil of spikenard. This precious ointment was used for burial of the dead. Its sweet aroma was Jesus' anointing for burial.

1. Who criticized Mary's lovely act of worship?

12:4-6 _____

2. Who defended her act of worship?

12:7, 8 _____

3. How effective was the testimony of Lazarus?

12:11 _____

On the next day, Jesus rode into Jerusalem. In that age, warlike kings and chieftains rode on horses. But Jesus rode into the city on an ass's colt, for He is the King of Peace. Lining the streets of the city, the multitude hailed Jesus as King. Little did they realize that His kingdom is not of this world but is in the hearts of men.

4. How did the people demonstrate their enthusiasm?

12:13 _____

5. How do we know that the fame of Jesus had reached the ears of the Gentiles?

12:20-21 _____

_____

6. By what analogy did Jesus suggest His coming death?

12:24 _____

7. In what words did He foretell that His death would be by crucifixion?

12:32 _____

8. What does 12:37 tell us about the efficacy of miracles to produce belief?

12:37 _____

9. There were some among the Pharisees who apparently believed in Jesus but did not confess Him openly. Why?

12:43 _____

10. In what words did the Lord describe His mission to this earth?

12:46 _____

11. Jesus did not claim to speak in His own authority. In whose authority did He speak?

12:49 _____

In John 12:44-50 we have Jesus' last appeal to the general public to believe on Him. Most of the religious leaders had turned their backs on even the evidence of his raising a man who had been dead four days, and were plotting to kill Jesus.

The Washing: "The Disciples' Feet" (chapter 13)

Jesus knew that He had only a short time left to spend with His little flock, so He withdrew from the public. In chapters 13 through 17 we find Him alone with His disciples.

12. Who was behind Judas Iscariot's dastardly betrayal of Jesus?

13:2 _____

13. What significant thing did Jesus do after supper?

13:4, 5 _____

14. Why did the Lord perform this humble service?

13:16, 17 _____

This section opens with an act of service—Jesus washes His disciples' feet. The teaching is clear: those who follow such a Master must serve one another as He served them. The disciple is *saved* in order that he may *serve*.

15. What statement from the Psalms was fulfilled at that supper?

13:18 _____

16. In what plain words did Jesus reveal His knowledge of His betrayer?

13:26 _____

17. What were the Lord's first words after Judas left the room?

13:31 _____

18. What new commandment did Jesus give His disciples?

13:34 _____

19. About what did He caution Peter?

13:38 _____

Complete the following sentences:

20. For the poor always ye have with you; _____

_____ 12:8

21. He that _____ his life shall _____; and

he that _____ his life in this world shall keep it

unto _____ 12:25

22. And he that seeth me seeth _____

_____ 12:45

23. Peter saith unto him, Thou shalt never wash my feet. Jesus

answered him, _____

_____

_____ 13:8

24. By this shall all men know that ye are my disciples, _____

_____ 13:35

25. Whither I go, thou canst not follow me now; but _____

_____ 13:36

Jesus made a last appeal to Judas by marking him out for a special favor. It was customary for a host to show special favor to one of his guests by dipping a choice morsel into the dish and then handing it to him. Jesus did that to Judas although He knew he was planning to betray Him.

After Satan entered into Judas, he "went immediately out; and it was night." Judas left the Light of Life for the darkness of despair.

Prayer: Dear Lord, keep me from denying Thee by word or deed. Help me to be a living witness for Thee today wherever I am.

You have just studied some important truths about John 12 and 13. Review your study by rereading the questions and your written answers. If you aren't sure of an answer, reread the Scripture portion given to see if you can find the answer. Then take the following test to see how well you understand important truths you have studied.

In the right-hand margin write "True" or "False" after each of the following statements.

1. Mary used a pound of ointment of spikenard to anoint the feet of Jesus. _____

2. The day after the anointing Jesus entered Jerusalem. _____

3. Jesus rode into the city on a white horse. _____

4. When people heard the voice from heaven they said it thundered. _____

5. Many of the people believed on Jesus because of the miracles. _____

6. Peter objected when Jesus began to wash his feet. _____

7. Judas, who later betrayed Jesus, was at the supper. _____

8. The disciples knew all along who the traitor was. _____

9. Jesus gave them a new commandment to love one another. _____

10. Peter said he would lay down his life for the Lord. _____

Turn to page 64 and check your answers.

The Comforter

JOHN, chapter 14

Divine Comfort: "The Holy Ghost"

Jesus was soon to depart out of the world, and He wished to prepare His disciples for that. The traitor had gone out into the night to tell Christ's enemies where they might find Him. With the little band of faithful ones gathered around Him, Jesus shared some of the things that were on His heart. His concern was not for Himself, but for those men whom He loved and was soon to leave.

Complete the following statements:

1. Ye believe in God _____ 14:1

2. And if I go and prepare a place for you _____

_____ 14:3

3. Jesus saith unto him, "I am _____

_____ 14:6

Knowing that He would be snatched from His disciples that very night, Jesus counseled them to have faith. He uttered the sixth "I AM"—I AM the way, the truth, and the life: no man cometh unto the Father, but by me." These words have been a comfort to all those who have put their trust in Christ, and an offense to those who have not. Jesus did not say that He was a way to God: He said He was the only way.

4. To whom was Jesus speaking when He claimed to be the way, the truth, and the life?

14:5 _____

5. If we really know Jesus, whom else will we know?

14:7, 9 _____

6. What has Jesus promised we can do if we believe in Him?

14:12 _____

7. What encouragement to pray does Christ give believers?

14:13 _____

8. What is the test of our love for Christ?

14:15 _____

9. Whom did Christ say He would pray the Father to give us?

14:16 _____

10. Who is this Comforter?

14:17 _____

Complete the following statements:

11. Because I live, _____ 14:19

12. At that day ye shall know that _____

_____ 14:20

13. He that loveth me shall be loved _____

_____ 14:21

14. If a man love me, he will keep my words: and my Father will

love him, _____ 14:23

38

15. What are two of the things the Holy Spirit does for us?

14:26 _____

16. What does Christ give us that the world cannot give?

14:27 _____

One of the greatest mysteries the Bible sets forth is that God is three Persons and yet only One. These persons are the Father, the Son, and the Holy Spirit. We say that God is a Trinity, or Three-in-One. In this fourteenth chapter you see how close is the inter-relationship of the Father, the Son, and the Holy Spirit. Jesus says, "He that hath seen me hath seen the Father." And He promises that in the coming of the Comforter, He Himself will come to His disciples.

17. What would the disciples do when the promise of the Comforter was fulfilled?

14:29 _____

God is beyond our understanding. He does not ask us to fully understand Him but to love and obey Him and to believe what He has revealed about Himself.

Meditate on Jesus' question to Philip: "Have I been so long time with you, and yet hast thou not known me?" Remind yourself of how long you have known Christ, and ask yourself how well you should know Him.

Prayer: Father, I thank you that my body is the temple of the Holy Spirit. Help me to always accept and obey the things He teaches me.

You have just studied some important truths about John 14. Review your study by rereading the questions and your written answers. If you aren't sure of an answer, reread the Scripture portion given to see if you can find the answer. Then take the following test to see how well you understand important truths you have studied.

In the right-hand margin write "True" or "False" after each of the following statements.

1. Jesus went to prepare a place for us. _____

2. Philip wanted Jesus to show him the Father. _____

3. He who believes on Jesus will do greater works than He did. _____

4. Answers to prayer glorify God through the Son. _____

5. Jesus refers to the Holy Spirit as the Spirit of Conquest. _____

6. He who loves the Lord Jesus will be loved by the world. _____

7. The Holy Ghost is called also the Comforter. _____

8. The peace of the world is like the peace that Jesus gives. _____

9. Satan is called the Prince of this world. _____

10. Obedience to the Father's command proved the love of Jesus for the Father. _____

Turn to page 64 and check your answers.

The True Vine

JOHN, chapter 15

The Vine: "Abide in Me"

In 14:20 Jesus says to His disciples, "Ye in me, and I in you." Now He uses the picture of the vine to describe the relationship between Himself and His disciples by saying, "I Am the Vine, ye are the branches." This is the seventh "I AM."

Fill in the missing words:

1. I am the _____, and my Father is the _____ 15:1

2. Every branch that beareth _____, he purgeth it, that

it may _____ 15:2

3. _____ in me, and I in _____ 15:4

4. He that abideth in me, and I in him, the same bringeth forth

_____; for without me ye can do _____ 15:5

5. If ye abide in me, and my words abide in you, ye shall ask

_____, and it shall be _____ 15:7

6. Herein is my Father glorified, that ye _____

_____; so shall ye be my disciples. 15:8

7. These things have I spoken unto you, that my _____

might remain in you, and that your _____ might be full.
15:11

8. These things I command you, that _____ 15:17

9. The servant is not greater than his _____ 15:20

10. He that hateth me hateth _____ 15:23

11. What is the only way for a Christian to bear spiritual fruit?

15:4 _____

12. What glorifies God?

15:8 _____

13. What does God use to cleanse a Christian for fruit bearing?

15:3 _____

14. How does a believer abide in Christ's love?

15:10 _____

15. How has Christ shown the greatness of His love to us?

15:13 _____

16. What is the world's attitude toward Christians and Christ?

15:18 _____

17. What is it that really condemns the world?

15:22 _____

18. To whom do both the Comforter and the Christian testify?

15:26, 27 _____

Memorize this wonderful verse:

"Ye have not chosen me, but I have chosen you, and ordained you, that ye should go and bring forth fruit, and that your fruit should remain: that whatsoever ye shall ask of the Father in my name, He may give it you." John 15:16

Prayer: Dear Father in heaven, may the fruit of the Spirit be seen in my character and the fruit of the harvest in my witness; for your great glory. Amen.

check-up time No. 9

You have just studied some important truths about John 15. Review your study by rereading the questions and your written answers. If you aren't sure of an answer, reread the Scripture portion given to see if you can find the answer. Then take the following test to see how well you understand important truths you have studied.

In the right-hand margin write "True" or "False" after each of the following statements.

1. Jesus is the true Vine, and the disciples are the husbandmen. _____

2. The Word of God has cleansing power. _____

3. The believer is the branch that receives life from the Vine. _____

4. Abiding in the Vine is vital to answered prayer. _____

5. Christ has shown His love for us by dying for us. _____

6. Jesus calls His followers His servants. _____

7. Believers are chosen and ordained to bring forth fruit. _____

8. The world loves the followers of Christ. _____

9. The Jews saw and hated Jesus. _____

10. The Spirit of Truth bears testimony of Christ. _____

Turn to page 64 and check your answers.

Persecution and Prayer

JOHN, chapters 16 and 17

Persecution: "Ye Shall Have Tribulation"
(chapter 16)

Jesus continued to warn, teach, and encourage His disciples. He said that it was better for Him to go away so that He could send the Holy Spirit in His place. He also warned them to expect persecution from the world.

1. What will be the sad thing about much persecution?

16:2 _____

2. What is the basic reason for this persecution?

16:3 _____

Let us see what part the Holy Spirit has in man's salvation. He reproves the world of sin, righteousness, and judgment. Men scoff at the seriousness of sin, have no desire for righteousness, and ignore coming judgment. When the Holy Spirit "reproves" such a one of sin, the conscience is pricked, and he calls upon God for cleansing and forgiveness.

3. On what ground does the Holy Spirit convict men and women of the following? 16:9-11

a. Sin _____

b. Righteousness _____

_____

c. Judgment _____

_____

The Holy Spirit continues His work in the believer, leading him into all truth and revealing Christ to him. Blessed Comforter, who first leads us to Christ and then helps us to grow in the spiritual life!

4. Into what does the Holy Spirit lead the believer?

16:13 _____

5. Whom does He glorify?

16:14 _____

Believer, the Holy Spirit is God's gift to you. Listen to His voice. Yield yourself to His leading and His infilling. He is your Comforter and Guide.

6. Why does the Father love each believer?

16:27 _____

7. What did Jesus foretell of the disciples' failure in the coming time of testing?

16:32 _____

8. Why did Jesus tell them this?

16:33 _____

9. Why does the Christian not need to fear the world's hatred?

16:33 _____

Prayer: "I Pray for Them" (chapter 17)

Jesus prayed for the disciples He was soon to leave. This beautiful prayer has been a source of comfort and strength for Christians down through the centuries.

10. What prompted this prayer?

17:1 _____

11. How did the Lord define the way of salvation?

17:3 _____

12. For whom did Christ pray?

17:9 _____

13. What specific request did Christ make for His own?

17:11 _____

14. In what way is the Christian to share in Christ's mission?

17:18 _____

Christians find that Christ was praying not only for the men and women who followed Him while He was on earth but "for them also which shall believe on me through their word."

15. If you are a believer, were you included in Christ's prayer?

17:20 _____

16. In this prayer was Christ bemoaning the cross or anticipating His glory?

17:24 _____

17. What descriptive word (if any) does Christ use of His Father when speaking to Him of

a. Himself—17:5 _____

b. His own—17:11 _____

c. The world—17:25 _____

If you belong to Christ, remember always that He prayed this for you. If you do not belong to Him, you can receive Him as your Lord and Saviour right where you are.

Fill in the missing words:

18. It is _____ for you that I go away: for if I go

not away, the _____ will not come unto you. 16:7

19. Hitherto have ye asked nothing in my name: ask, and ye shall

receive _____ 16:24

20. I have _____ thee on the earth: I have

_____ the work which _____ gavest
me to do. 17:4

21. For I have given unto them _____

which thou gavest me; and they have _____
them. 17:8

22. Holy Father, keep through thine own name _____

_____ as we are. 17:11

23. I pray not that Thou shouldest _____,

but that Thou shouldest _____ 17:15

24. Neither pray I for these alone, but for _____

_____ through their word. 17:20

25. That the world may know that _____, and

hast loved them, as _____ 17:23

26. That the love wherewith thou _____

may be in them, and I in them. 17:26

Memorize this great definition of eternal life:

"And this is life eternal, that they might know thee the only true God, and Jesus Christ, whom thou hast sent." 17:3

Prayer: Thank You, Lord Jesus, that You have given me your word, and I have received it and believed. Now keep me true to You.

check-up time No. 10

You have just studied some important truths about John 16 and 17. Review your study by rereading the questions and your written answers. If you aren't sure of an answer, reread the Scripture portion given to see if you can find the answer. Then take the following test to see how well you understand the important truths you have studied.

In the right-hand margin write "True" or "False" after each of the following statements.

1. The followers of Jesus will be welcomed by all. _____

2. Jesus had to leave the earth before the Comforter could come. _____

3. Before Jesus left the disciples He guided them into all truth. _____

4. The Lord said that the world would sorrow over His death. _____

5. The Lord said that the disciples would be popular in the world after the resurrection. _____

6. The Father gave the Son power over all flesh. _____

7. Jesus finished the work that the Father gave Him to do. _____

8. Jesus prayed for the entire world. _____

9. As the Father sent the Son, so the Son sent His followers into the world. _____

10. All the world knows God. _____

Turn to page 64 and check your answers.

The Cup and the Cross

JOHN, chapters 18 and 19

The cup: "Shall I Not Drink It?" (chapter 18)

According to the laws of the Jews, a blasphemer should be put to death. The Jews called Jesus a blasphemer because He spoke of Himself as the Son of God.

1. Who came to arrest the Lord?

18:3 _____

2. What did the Lord say to Peter when he tried to defend Him with carnal weapons?

18:11 _____

3. Who was Caiaphas?

18:13-14 _____

4. What did Jesus say when His captors demanded that He explain His doctrine?

18:20-21 _____

_____

_____

Only a Roman official could authorize a man's being put to death. Therefore, after condemning Jesus in their own courts, the Jewish leaders took Him to the Roman official Pilate to have him pronounce the death sentence. Pilate could see no reason why Jesus should be put to death and tried to release Him.

51

5. What important question did Pilate put to Christ?

18:33 _____

6. In what words did Christ lay claim to absolute Sovereignty?

18:37 _____

7. What was Pilate's assessment of the charges brought against Christ?

18:38 _____

8. Whom did the Jews prefer to Christ?

18:39, 40 _____

In this chapter we see the beginning of the fulfillments of Christ's prophecy in 16:32, "Ye shall be scattered and leave me alone." Judas betrayed Him, and Peter denied that he was one of Christ's disciples. Would fear make you disloyal to Jesus Christ?

The Crucifixion: "It Is Finished" (chapter 19)

The nineteenth chapter of John's gospel brings us to the darkest hour in the history of the world since the day that sin first entered the human race. The pure, holy, spotless Son of God was rejected by those who should have loved and honored Him.

9. What brutal thing did Pilate do to the Man he had just pronounced innocent?

19:1-3 _____

10. How did the Jewish leaders give vent to their hatred of Christ?

19:6 _____

11. Did the Jewish leaders understand that Christ claimed to be God?

19:7 _____

12. When Pilate finally gave in to the mob, where did they take Him to crucify Him?

19:17 _____

He was betrayed by justice and deserted by His friends. He was delivered into the hands of His enemies and was subjected to the death that the Romans meted out to the worst criminals. He Who had come from the highest had now stooped to the lowest, the shameful death of the cross.

13. What was the formal accusation nailed to Christ's cross?

19:19 _____

14. Which Old Testament prophecy was fulfilled unconsciously by the soldiers who executed Christ?

19:24 _____

_____

15. Why did Christ say, "I thirst"?

19:28 _____

16. What Old Testament Scripture did the soldiers unconsciously fulfill when they refrained from breaking Christ's legs?

19:31-37 _____

It looked like defeat, and yet it was for this purpose that He had come into the world. Jesus said, "For this cause came I unto this hour" (12:27). "I lay down my life for the sheep . . . no man taketh it from me, but I lay it down of myself" (10:15, 18), "Even so must the Son of man be lifted up, that whosoever believeth in Him should not perish, but have everlasting life" (3:14-15).

53

17. Where was Christ buried?

19:38-42 _____

Through jealousy the Jews had Jesus crucified. They planned evil against Him, but God meant it for good. Christ paid the price for the salvation of all who would put their trust in Him. Jesus "bare our sins in His own body on the tree . . . For Christ also hath once suffered for sins, the just for the unjust, that He might bring us to God" (1 Peter 2:24; 3:18). He died for your sins.

Complete the following sentences:

18. As soon as he had said unto them, I am he, they went

backward _____ 18:6

19. Then saith the damsel that kept the door unto Peter, Art not

thou also one of this man's disciples? He saith, _____

_____ 18:17

20. Jesus answered, My kingdom _____ 18:36

21. Pilate . . . went out again unto the Jews and saith unto them, I

find _____ 18:38

22. The Jews answered him, We have a law, and by our law he

ought to die, because _____ 19:7

23. Jesus answered, Thou couldest have no power at all against

me, except _____ 19:11

24. Pilate saith unto them, Shall I crucify your King? The chief

priests answered, We have _____ 19:15

25. When Jesus therefore had received the vinegar, he said, ___

_____ 19:30

26. These things were done, that the scripture should be fulfilled,

_____ 19:36

27. And again another scripture saith, They shall _____

_____ 19:37

You have just studied some important truths about
John 18 and 19. Review your study by rereading
the questions and your written answers. If you
aren't sure of an answer, reread the Scripture portion given to see if you can find the answer. Then
take the following test to see how well you understand important truths you have studied.

*In the right-hand margin write "True" or "False"
after each of the following statements.*

1. Andrew fought with his sword to protect the
Lord Jesus. _____

2. Peter went in before the high priest to defend
Jesus. _____

3. Peter warmed himself at the fire of coals. _____

4. Peter confessed that he was a follower of Jesus. _____

5. The kingdom that Jesus was talking about is not
of this world. _____

6. Pilate could find no fault in the Lord Jesus. _____

7. The chief priests refused to recognize Christ as
king. _____

8. Jesus was crucified at a place called "the skull." _____

9. The mother of Jesus deserted Him when He was
crucified. _____

10. Nicodemus helped prepare the body of Jesus for
burial. _____

Turn to page 64 and check your answers.

Resurrection and Resolution

JOHN, chapters 20 and 21

The Resurrection: "He Must Rise" (chapter 20)

The disciples were dazed and grief-stricken because of the death of their Lord. But now came the news that electrified them! The tomb was empty, except for the graveclothes. A woman reported that she had seen Him alive. Hope began to rise, and the words they had not understood at the time began to stir in their minds: "Destroy this temple, and in three days I will raise it up" (2:19). "I lay down my life, that I might take it again" (10:17).

1. Who was the first person to tell of the empty tomb?

20:1-2 _____

2. Which two disciples ran to the empty tomb to investigate for themselves?

20:3 _____ and _____

3. What word did Jesus use to prove to Mary Magdalene that His body had not been stolen and that He was risen indeed?

20:11-16 _____

On the cross Jesus had said, "It is finished." He had paid the price for our redemption. For thirty-three years He had lived the spotless, blameless life that we all have failed to live; then on the cross He offered up that holy life to atone for our sinfulness. When He shed His blood for sinful men and women, the great sacrifice was finished that makes it possible for all who believe to come to God. And yet one thing remained—He must rise from the dead.

4. Where were the disciples when the Lord appeared to the group?

20:19-20 _____

If Christ had remained in the power of death, all hope of salvation through Him would be vain. If death could have held Him, He would have been shown to be only a man. No man could have redeemed a fallen world; only the infinite life of God Himself is sufficient to redeem millions. But Christ did rise, victor over death. Hallelujah, what a Savior!

5. What was the Lord's commission to His own?

20:21 _____

6. How did Christ convince skeptical Thomas of the reality of His literal resurrection?

20:24-28 _____

_____

7. What was John's main purpose in writing this gospel?

20:31 _____

_____

_____

8. Has this gospel accomplished its purpose in your life?

_____

The Son of God had died for sins and risen again. Paul says, "I declare unto you the gospel . . . by which also ye are saved . . . Christ died for our sins according to the Scriptures; He was buried, and He rose again the third day according to the Scriptures" (1 Corinthians 15:1-4). This is the message Christ's followers must preach: "Repent, and believe the gospel. Believe that the Son of God died for you and rose again."

Resolution: "Follow Me" (chapter 21)

Two things transformed the disciples-the knowledge that their Lord had conquered death and the coming into their lives of the Holy Spirit. They fearlessly faced persecution and death. They scattered and hid when He was arrested.

9. What other incident connected with the resurrection does John record?

21:1 _____

10. Who was the first to recognize the risen Christ on this occasion?

21:7 _____

11. How many times did the Lord ask Peter if he loved Him?

21:15-17 _____

The disciples had not yet set out to preach. They were still too stunned by the recent events and needed time to comprehend their meaning. They had received the Holy Spirit (20:22), but they would not receive His anointing with power for some days yet. They then would go forth as flaming evangelists.

12. How does John designate himself throughout this gospel?

21:20 _____

13. How do we know it was John who wrote this gospel?

21:24 _____

14. Do the gospels tell us *all* that Jesus said and did?

21:25 _____

The unnamed disciple tells us that he is the one who wrote this account of the life of Christ (21:24). What modesty John shows in not naming himself as the writer. What great love he must have had for

59

his Lord to stand with the little group of mourning women at the cross rather than fleeing to safety. "Perfect love casteth out fear."

Complete the following sentences:

15. Then went in also that other disciple, which came first to the

sepulchre, and _____ 20:8

16. Go to my brethren, and say unto them, I ascend unto my

_____ _____ 20:17

17. Then said Jesus to them again, Peace be unto you: as my

Father has sent me, _____ 20:21

18. And Thomas answered and said unto him, _____

_____ 20:28

19. And he said unto them, Cast _____

_____ 21:6

20. This is now _____ that Jesus shewed himself to his disciples, after that he was risen from the dead. 21:14

21. This spake he signifying by what death he [Peter] should

_____ 21:19

22. Jesus saith unto him, If I will that he tarry till I come, what is

that to thee? _____ 21:22

"BUT THESE ARE WRITTEN, THAT YE MIGHT BELIEVE THAT JESUS IS THE CHRIST, THE SON OF GOD; AND THAT BELIEVING YE MIGHT HAVE LIFE THROUGH HIS NAME." (John 20:31)

Prayer: Dear Lord, as I come to the end of this brief study of John's gospel, cause me to believe what I have studied and to obey what I have believed.

check-up time No. 12

You have just studied some important truths about John 20 and 21. Review your study by rereading the questions and your written answers. If you aren't sure of an answer, reread the Scripture portion given to see if you can find the answer. Then take the following test to see how well you understand important truths you have studied.

In the right-hand margin write "True" or "False" after each of the following statements.

1. Peter was the first one to visit the sepulcher of Jesus. _____

2. Two angels were at the tomb to tell about Jesus. _____

3. Mary Magdalene came and told the disciples that she had seen the Lord. _____

4. The disciples were glad when they saw the Lord. _____

5. Thomas was the first to believe that Jesus had risen. _____

6. Simon Peter went back to his fishing business. _____

7. The disciples caught no fish at all on that fishing trip. _____

8. This was the second time Jesus had shown Himself to the disciples. _____

9. Jesus told Peter to feed His sheep. _____

10. John's purpose in writing was that people might believe in Christ and thus be saved. _____

Turn to page 64 and check your answers.

Suggestions for class use

1. The class teacher may wish to tear this page from each workbook as the answer key is on the reverse side.

2. The teacher should study the lesson first, filling in the blanks in the workbook. He should be prepared to give help to the class on some of the harder places in the lesson. He should also take the self-check tests himself, check his answers with the answer key, and look up any question answered incorrectly.

3. Class sessions can be supplemented by the teacher's giving a talk or leading a discussion on the subject to be studied. The class could then fill in the workbook together as a group, in teams, or individually. If so desired by the teacher, however, this could be done at home. The self-check tests can be done as homework by the class.

4. The self-check tests may be corrected at the beginning of each class session. A brief discussion of the answers can serve as review for the previous lesson.

5. The teacher should motivate and encourage his students. Some public recognition might well be given to class members who successfully complete this course.

Moody Press, a ministry of the Moody Bible Institute is designed for education, evangelization, and edification. If we may assist you in knowing more about Christ and the Christian life, please write without obligation to:.
Moody Press, c/o MLM, Chicago, Illinois 60610

answer key
to self-check tests

Be sure to look up any questions you answered incorrectly.

Q gives the number of the test *question*.

A gives the correct *answer*.

R *refers* you back to the chapter and verse in the gospel of John, where the correct answer is to be found.

Mark with an "x" your wrong answers.

Q	TEST 1 A	R	TEST 2 A	R	TEST 3 A	R	TEST 4 A	R	TEST 5 A	R	TEST 6 A	R
1	F	1:29	F	2:1	F	4:5	F	6:13	F	8:11	T	10:16
2	T	1:34	T	2:11	T	4:10	T	6:17	T	8:19	T	10:15
3	F	1:26	F	2:13	F	4:24	T	6:19	F	8:31	F	10:18
4	T	1:24	F	2:15	T	4:39	F	6:48	F	8:36	F	10:26
5	F	1:21	T	2:23	T	4:50	F	6:66	T	8:56	F	10:31
6	T	1:32	T	3:1	F	5:2	F	6:70	F	9:7	F	11:6
7	F	1:40	F	3:3	T	5:14	T	7:10	T	9:20	T	11:8
8	T	1:45	F	3:14	T	5:22	F	7:13	F	9:28	F	11:20
9	T	1:49	T	3:24	F	5:36	T	7:39	T	9:34	T	11:27
10	T	1:50	T	3:28	F	5:39	F	7:40	T	9:37	T	11:51

Q	TEST 7 A	R	TEST 8 A	R	TEST 9 A	R	TEST 10 A	R	TEST 11 A	R	TEST 12 A	R
1	T	12:3	T	14:2	F	15:1	F	16:2	F	18:10	F	20:1
2	T	12:12	T	14.8	T	15:3	T	16:7	F	18:16	T	20:12
3	F	12:15	T	14:12	T	15:5	F	16:13	T	18:18	T	20:18
4	T	12:29	T	14:13	T	15:7	F	16:20	F	18:25	T	20:20
5	F	12:37	F	14:17	T	15:13	F	16:33	T	18:36	F	20:25
6	T	13:6	F	14:21	F	15:15	T	17:2	T	19:6	T	21:3
7	T	13:18	T	14:26	T	15:16	T	17:4	T	19:15	F	21:6
8	F	13:22	F	14:27	F	15:19	F	17:9	T	19:17	F	21:14
9	T	13:34	T	14:30	T	15:24	T	17:18	F	19:25	T	21:16
10	T	13:37	T	14:31	T	15:26	F	17:25	T	19:39	T	20:31

How well did you do?

0-1 wrong answers—excellent work

2-3 wrong answers—review errors carefully

4 or more wrong answers—restudy the lesson before going on to the next one